AFTERMATH

Aftermath

Thomas March

THE HILARY THAM CAPITAL COLLECTION
2018 Selections by Joan Larkin

THE WORD WORKS
WASHINGTON, D.C.

The Word Works
P.O. Box 42164
Washington, D.C. 20015
editor@wordworksbooks.org

Cover art: Michael Eirhart
"Untitled." Watercolor on archival cold-press paper.
Cover design: Susan Pearce Design
Author photograph: Matt O'Brien

ISBN: 978-1-944585-20-4
LCCN: 2018931393

Acknowledgments

88: A Journal of Contemporary American Poetry: "At the Quaker Meeting House"

Assaracus: "Aubade, Too Early" (reprint), "Kissing Jake at a Wedding," "The Love Lives of the Castrati," "Photograph of Jake at Nineteen," and "St. Sebastian to the One Who Fired First"

Bellevue Literary Review: "Aubade, Too Early," and "The Barn"

BETWEEN: New Gay Poetry (Chelsea Station Editions): "The Wedding Reception Ends"

Boston Literary Magazine: "Sick Child on an Elevator"

Chelsea Station: "At the Lake, Later"

Confrontation: "Summer City Morning, After a Sudden Storm"

GLASS: A Journal of Poetry: "My Mother Knew How"

Heliotrope: "Brief (Enough) Encounter" (reprint)

HIV Here and Now: "Ideal Weight"

Hunger Mountain Review: "The Hole I Dug"

Kin: "Near First Avenue, After the Hurricane, 2012"

Noon: Journal of the Short Poem: "4 a.m." and "There Have Been No Accidents/Injuries at This Worksite in [79] Days"

Poetic Voices Without Borders 2 (Gival Press): "Virginia Woolf's Pockets, Full of Stones"

Public Pool: "Never the Belt," "The Sacrifice of Isaac," and "Your T-Shirt"

Red Poppy Review: "Brief (Enough) Encounter"

RHINO: "Ideal Weight"

The Account: "Instead"

The Common Online: "In the Apartment, After You've Gone," and "Morning (After) Commute"

The Gay and Lesbian Review: "Swapping Gum"

The Good Men Project: "After I Watched *The Deer Hunter*"

The Ledge Poetry and Fiction Magazine: "Fireflies"

The Q Review: "My First Drunk, 17" & "Pallbearers for Our Favorite Drunk"

The Spoon River Poetry Review: "Edward Hopper's '7 a.m.'"

Vallum: "The Raided Nest"

Vanilla: "Second Night"

Writer's Ink: "From His Deathbed," and "Sonnet in Trimeter"

When you are in your 40s when you publish your first book of poems, there are many people to thank.

For time and other resources, I am grateful to the Brearley School professional development fund, Lambda Literary, the Millay Colony for the Arts, and Vermont Studio Center.

For selecting *Aftermath*, I am grateful to Joan Larkin, and for taking very good care of it, I am grateful to Nina Budabin McQuown and Nancy White.

For their helpful thoughts or suggestions on work that appears in this book, in whole or in part, I am grateful to Fanny Howe, Marie Howe, Glyn Maxwell, Jerome Murphy, Elizabeth Richards, Jason Schneiderman, Katherine Swett, and A. Van Jordan.

For their support and fellowship, I am grateful to my colleagues at the Brearley School, William Johnson, and The Theaterists.

For their wicked mirth and kind conspiracy, I thank Tyler Mills and Susan Steinberg.

I am indebted to my teachers, most especially Joanne Andrews. Whatever generosity or wisdom I'm able to manifest in my own teaching extends from her example.

For always believing, I'm grateful to Vina March. For their love and a lifetime of good lessons, I am grateful to my parents, Tom and Dawn March; and to my grandparents, Betty and Don Marcy.

And for his faith, love, wit, generous spirit, and so much else, I am grateful to Joshua Padgett.

Contents

Aftermath

After Orlando

St. Sebastian to the One Who Fired First

You had to pierce me first, your arrow sure
to prove yourself again against my skin.
The others follow swift and unaware
that with each pinch, each plunge, I testify—
but even as they mitigate my breath
there's no undoing what the tongue has done
—the truth you know we two have come to know:
not just that God is love but love is God.
For that, your arrow breaks against the bone.
For that, you miss your mark, to leave me here
to live, lament and die. But not today.

After Orlando

for J.H.P.

Two men embrace somewhere, beneath
the hard Pompeiian ash, surprised
by a blasting, rushing darkness.

If we're together at the end,
could either of us close our eyes
against the other's dying face?

If one of us should look away,
could we see each other again
unfleshed? And would we recognize

each other if our ash remained
unmixed, because they'd buried us
as if we'd lived only apart?

Would you forgive my dying first
if my last breath announced your name
ahead of mine, to hold your place?

I ask you this understanding
promises are best intentions
and only the comfort of now.

My First Drunk, 17

At parties, I would watch him lean
against the boys who bore his weight
so easily against their own
for hours before I helped him home—
but never to the narrow bed
where no one waited up to hold his head.

And then, behind my backyard steps,
we'd huddle—safe in shadow—he'd
produce his flask of pilfered gin,
watching me as he offered it,
as if I might not drink enough.
He wouldn't wipe its mouth when it returned.

Just once, I kept his pace but kept
my sips as shallow as my breath
was deep, until he slurred the words
that always came—when he would bend
to whisper in my ear, confess
his simple love with sober-seeming calm—

his drunkenness an alibi
that I was ready to destroy
by intercepting him, to force
a single accidental touch.
Instead, he shuddered as the gin
returned beneath a froth of friendly beers.

What could I do but take him in
to lie across the bathroom floor?
I cocked his head to keep his sick

from choking him. Then I leaned hard
against the toilet's clammy rim,
as if to transfer all its cool to him.

Photograph of Jake at Nineteen

When he stayed past our hangovers, I knew—
with boldness born of boredom—he'd consent,
if only for the sake of art, to pose,
to be my model for the afternoon.
But I stepped in too close for this last shot
to catch the best exposure I had planned—

the box I posed him on was low—his legs
splay wide, beyond the frame—his feet are gone,
and all the light I aimed his way was wrong.
So shadows fill the space between his knees
to stain his favorite lightly-faded jeans.
As he bends forward, elbows on his thighs,

through smoke that curls up from the cigarette
I lit for him, it's possible to see,
on his right hand, the number and the name
of one more girl he'd never call. Instead—
I was the only one who could know why—
he turns his head but cannot look away.

Swapping Gum

It was the closest we could come
to being together at school,
swapping gum in the halls, our hands
sloppy with syrup and our spit,
saving flavor—
                    it was so sweet,
sweet, fellow fool—what did we know
of the dark dangers of sharing?

Sonnet in Trimeter

The morning I left town,
I saw it on the tracks—
the bottle we drank down,
to ease us on our backs.

If it no longer stood,
I'd let our goodbye stand.
But you made sure it would.
You steadied it with sand.

I could have let it pass—
considered it a sweet
coincidence in glass
and gravel from the street—

no more than I could stay—
the weight of waking day.

At the Lake, Later

This lake was once a safer place.
You couldn't hear these highway sounds
that whir above the cricket calls
that used to supplement our shouts
and splashing, in the low sly burn
of dock lights, when the denser dark
of trees across the cove stretched past
our care. But now the headlights there
intrude through bramble swaying in
the wakes of trucks that draw the wind away.

Sometimes a boat would interrupt
our swim, announce itself before
it turned the corner, with a purr
we felt vibrating through our legs.
Until the choppy waves relaxed,
restoring our calm solitude,
we'd huddle underneath this dock
and, in the darker shallows there,
cling loosely, quiet, to the poles
as cold waves pressed us close in woody air.

Our last night was as other nights.
We floated far from shore, but when
I stretched my legs down to the mud,
it rooted me, that night, too slow
to dodge the unexpected lunge
that I mistook for eagerness
and courage—as he tackled me.
I plunged so fast my lungs were full—
my hand had only brushed his leg—
before he finished swimming over me.

In my brief yielding was enough
to cancel any coming back.
A squandered opportunity,
or unavoidable defeat,
it marked a silent fall, unknown
beyond this place or past that day.
Just as new moss along this dock
obscures the names we carved into
its sides, in separate silence, we
became the men we could not help but be.

Kissing Jake at a Wedding

The ice had melted as I held your drink
and you danced with your girlfriend—as you turned
I took some time to marinate and think
about the righteousness of favors earned.
So when you came to claim it, I could state
my humble fee, too drunk to hesitate:
you had to kiss me for it—and apply
some feeling, for the time that I'd stood by.

We kissed—with parted lips—and then, apart.
And with the ease that follows from relief,
you gently took your drink away, to start
another dance with her. But I believe
there's meaning in the pressure you applied,
the parted lips, the lingering collapse
into a smile (or smirk). But did a lapse
of caution—did I press too far?—decide

that we would share no more that night—at last—
we only had one beer-bold kiss. I tried
believing the weak contents of that glass
had caused your straying. But that kiss belied
the innocence with which you had returned.
So maybe you weren't wrong to go. I've learned
it isn't what I had or what I lack—
the cost of crossing was your crossing back.

Your T-Shirt

We earned our wounds those summer afternoons—
tackling each other, jumping, climbing things—
the worst was just a fall as we walked home.
I couldn't feel, until I saw your face—
the way confusion blossomed into shock
before contracting into cool concern—
the glass embedded deep, behind my knee.

I couldn't feel the blood until you pressed
your thumb against the inside of my leg
and eased the glass out with your other hand—
then, as the pooling thickness of my blood
diluted in the slickness of your sweat,
you took your t-shirt off and wrapped it tight
around my knee.

                And bearing half my weight
you helped me home—and carefully undressed
and dressed the wound again. Maybe you kissed
it once, before you taped the bandage on.
I might have kissed you better at the door.
Or that's a wish that only memory grants.

The scar is real but disappears—each year
it fades, just as your t-shirt has—and you
would never guess how well it fits me, still
a bloodstained totem of an old taboo.

The Love Lives of the Castrati

I.
They might have been relieved
when they were gone,

released into the praise
of other parts—

the fullness of the lungs,
the pounding heart,

a potency of voice
now unrestrained.

II.
How could they care for weight
that never weighed,

whose pendant urgencies
sway other men

from higher graces, Love's
more chaste pursuits?

But there's no surgery
to separate

III.
imagination from
the longing heart—

so no less forcefully
must they have met

this misery of age:
that one can mourn

what one has always missed
but never known.

After I Watched *The Deer Hunter*

Never the Belt

Never the belt—the belt
too like his own father
whose belt had its own name
that the whiskey gave it—
so never the whiskey
in the house, just the beer
for after the yard work—
but still, "Your ass is grass,
and I'm gonna mow it!"
when it would come to that.
Never the belt—instead
the ping pong paddle, wood
just firm and flexible
enough to sting, not bruise—
never branding the boy
(as he had been) as "boy,"
the name his father had
for whoever it was
tumbling through his vision—
and my padding myself
with wash cloths and even
paperback books (more like
a game than a beating)
until it was the books,
their shape and sound so sharp
there was no pretending.
Then we had to decide
how the next blow would fall—
full forward into farce
or back to the breaking
of paddles—in silence,
until I said, "I am

too old for this" and was.
So were we both too old
and so unlike his own
father, who didn't live
long enough for wisdom.
And so never the belt
or the paddle, either,
or calling a boy "boy,"
but his own name, only.

After I Watched *The Deer Hunter*

After I watched *The Deer Hunter*
thirty years later, I asked him,
my father, had it been like that,
because I recognized those streets
from my visits back home with him
and the ways of those wedding halls
and bows like those his father left,
whose razor-edged arrows he hid—
and because I had learned the smell
of frying deer there and had seen
a field-dressed carcass on a truck.

And because he knew what I knew—
that he spent the war repairing
bombers and not being shot at—
he knew what I was asking him
was not the usual question.
He said yes, it had been like that—
the way a long-known thing becomes
easy to say, if not to know.

And because this was on the phone
I couldn't see what else he felt
when I finally understood
why I never met any friends
of his, back in Pennsylvania.

My Mother Knew How

It could be fall
or early spring—
because her coat
is buttoned up
and there is wind
in some stray hairs
but no flinching—
in that photo
of my mother
by whoever
loved her that way
at seventeen,
a way that knew
that her eyes could
still dare him through
those thick glasses
and her half-smile
was just as much
as she could give
in confidence
and still take back.

Inheritance, Three Wrenches

I weighed eleven pounds—
at birth—that may be why
my grandfather believed
that I was destined to
be strong someday, a man
who'd never need to ask
someone else to fix things,
and he sent three wrenches
in an old chocolates box,
ready for me to lift
as soon as I could grip.
But I would never want
to tune engines. I'd have
preferred chocolates, instead
of wrenches and a wish
that I would take up tools.

At ten, though, I needed
the combination wrench
when my brother's skateboard
lost a wheel, and none of
his friends could replace it.

The adjustable wrench
stopped a fight at forty
when my boyfriend and I
lost our patience, trying
to assemble a couch.

I could, with the pipe wrench,
reverse a minor leak
if called on, to complete
my welcome to this world
that always wants repair.

The Sacrifice of Isaac

How could my faith ever have been his fault—
and who would ever look to be betrayed,
when love will leaven wariness with hope?

The bonds weren't necessary, just that bond
that made me see the shining blade as just
a test—of bravery and loyalty—the trust
a son should bear. But who, knowing favor,
when favor hadn't stopped the rising steel
could credit favor when it only fell
to slice beneath the ropes that held me still?

What was the magic in my lying down
that drew the knife back swiftly to his side?
It's something—being blessed by willingness—
it's something. But it doesn't bear relief.

The Hole I Dug

She chose an inconvenient time to die
but chose the warmest place there was, away
from the mossy tree where we kept her chained
for safety, so she wouldn't run away.
Her sharp sight wasted on our narrow yard,
she broke her rusty chain and stumbled near
the leafy hedge that framed the yard, to lie
alone in sunny silence, on her back.
From that last angle, she could not have seen
the hedge defended nothing interesting.

The first warm rain had softened up the ground.
I used the dulling shovel that we left
outside all winter, up against a shed.
The cold had warped the handle, and it shook
inside the rusty socket of the blade.
But it was all I had; I had to learn
to press my weight down carefully, to take
my shovelsful in shallow increments.
It took all afternoon to dig chest-deep
as every gentle pressure from my feet
disturbed the dirt that I had failed to lift—
but that was less time than she took to die,
the months of heavy hacking, every breath-
less howl announcing her impending death.

From digging in that shady spot, I knew
the smell of loneliness—the muddy food,
the acrid earth between the roots still damp
where she had overturned her water bowl.
I wished I could have killed her, slipped a pill

and held her still. She never would have had
to claim her freedom forcefully, or die
alone, where she had finally escaped
the shade, only to watch the sun so long
her tongue had swollen, and her eyes had dried.

Sick Child on an Elevator

Your shame has drained your face of all but fear
and the fluorescent gleam of clammy skin,
white as your knuckles on the garbage bin
you wrap your arms around as we ascend.

It might be some small comfort to believe
that nothing else could ever be as bad
as this uncertain certainty of sick.
But you must learn—as every lurch and heave

in our slow-seeming progress from the ground
prolongs your public suffering again—
how inconveniently the distance swells
between humiliation and relief.

Edward Hopper's "7 a.m."

"The clock says seven, but what time of day?"
the "Art Appreciation" lady asked.
She came on Tuesdays, every other week,
and knew us not by name but by our grade.
She held the mounted print upon her knees
and smiled a smile she seemed to wish we'd smile,
believing that this clock could tell our age.

I answered, "Morning!" But I don't know why.
I was no prodigy of painted light.
I had no special insight on the scene.
I saw what anybody else would see—
an empty store, its walls a dingy white,
a tidy dirt yard, then a depth of trees.

"How did you know?" she asked. I couldn't say—
except that people like that time of night,
and it's their lounging presence, not the light
that marks the falling hours of the day.
And maybe I saw signs of waking life
among the greens that smudge between the trees.

That was the time of day that I knew best.
I'd wake to make my breakfast by myself.
More than the light, the clock, the vacancy,
the out and upward yawn of trees, I knew
the burdensome proximity of dreams.

The Raided Nest

Her ritual of raiding was to wait
and watch until the young had fled their nests
and left behind their flattened, emptied shells.

She knew her catalog of trees as well
as every dusty corner of her room,
whose walls she decorated with the blues

of robins' eggs, mosaics of the sky
and, in the browns of sparrows' eggs, the ground.
She stepped barefoot onto the loamy earth;

around her toes it yielded as she stepped,
shaped by her silent, wary shifts of weight.
Then underneath a nest she'd known for weeks,

just low enough that she could reach its lip,
just high enough that she would have to stretch
to get at anything inside, she stopped

and wondered once again how from a twig
and just the proper yield of tree they wove
defenses and a balanced world of warmth.

When she reached in to pull the eggshells out
she felt the feathers, soft but flattened down
and dried, worm-eaten. Nothing would return.

She brought the whole nest to her waiting walls,
her years of cracked and reconnected shells.
She painted over eyes that never knew

the pastures' greens, the art of shaping earth
to fit their body's welfare and their world,
but knew instead too soon the mouldering brown.

Fireflies

We captured fistfuls in our cooling night
and held them just as everybody did,
in jars. The fireflies weren't very bright.
When they escaped the holes cut in the lid,
they couldn't fly fast or maintain their height.
To keep them close, my brother stripped their wings
and puffed away a lifetime's worth of flight
for half an hour of grounded, glaring things.
It was the most indecent kind of crime,
to concentrate their love-compelling light,
expose them to their mates, at mating time,
as feeble-flying—lacking enough might
to keep their wings, parade their love about,
then fly from their used lovers' prying sight.

So I would carve their glowing bellies out
and send them speechless back into the night.

Slugs

Begrudging them their undetermined shapes,
so useless in their iridescent turns,
which marred the clean concrete that would have cooked
them in the day but in the dark became
a stolen canvas for their shining slime,
the gleaming congealed trails they left behind—
each night, I ran for salt at my first sight
of them. I'd choose the fattest one to pour
it on, then watch it shrivel up, the life
escaping brown into the brilliant mound.
I often gave them extra time, to test
my art. I started pouring at the tail
then stopped midway to watch the living head
attempt to pull away, expand and fail
and then pulse full ahead, contracting back
untired, to try again, as if by will
it could reanimate its lower half.
Each morning I would spray their trails away.

But my grandmother had a better way.
She left out shallow tubs of beer, and in
the morning, they'd be full of slugs,
who'd soaked the sugars through their tender skin
and could not move for being overwhelmed
with flat, fermented sweetness, and so drowned.
One afternoon I helped her harvest beans,
as she collected slugs from several tubs.
She shook their bloated but coherent clods
of flesh and spread them in between the plants
to be of use in rotting toward the roots.
When we had turned our backs, my brother picked

one up and placed it in his sparse-toothed mouth.
His smile was tight, too full as we approached
him, quietly cross-legged on the ground.
We pried his mouth apart and found a slug
alive, somehow, not drunk enough to die.
I asked him later how it felt—and why
he hadn't bitten it in half; it stayed
immobile, on his tongue, he said, and all
he felt was tickling from antennae as
they gently probed the space between his teeth.

Somehow, it has survived, their probing calm,
indifferent to size and speed and those
who fear their jellied guts between our toes.
I've watched them from the top step of the porch
for hours, my ankles gray from garden work,
my bare feet cool against the bottom step.
The porch light draws the yard's more frantic beings
to smoky, violent deaths; the slugs just climb
the bottom step, investigate my feet
as one by one they come to telescope
their fleshy soft antennae through the gaps
between my toes, turn back, and let me be.
They linger and take time to notice well,
emboldened by their flexibility,
and by the early morning there will be
bright arcs that mark their every twisting glance,
their pearly trails a welcome record of
their caution and their curiosity.

After the Hurricane

Near First Avenue, After the Hurricane, 2012

And the voice of harpers, and musicians, and of pipers,
and trumpeters, shall be heard no more at all in thee; and no
craftsman, of whatsoever craft he be, shall be found any more
in thee. ——Revelation 18:22

It was strangely quiet
outside and in——music
was private, and the wind
less terrifying than
it might have been. We, who
had been prepared for more,
with guilt remained indoors
to gorge on unspoiled food.
We knew that we were bored.

But neither of us made
the effort to engage
in Scrabble, or in cards——
the work of building suits
or words demanded more
than there was power for.
Those days, we didn't know
the surging river's flow
had nearly reached our door.

Aubade: Too Early

No touch had been unwanted and no word
of urgency unuttered or unheard.
But still the silence came—and yet no snore.
I caught you staring out the bedroom door.

You couldn't stay this time, and you confessed
you had somewhere to be—and then you dressed.
Somewhere to be at three a.m.—not quite,
but in the morning, and to spend the night
would mean a hasty morning. You had planned
to cook for friends—you knew I'd understand—
to cook for friends whose names I'd never heard
and wasn't meant to meet. Without a word,
you smiled and kissed me sweetly, though—and thus
was I meant for the bed, you for the bus
and for a few untroubled hours, as I
stayed up to bring some daylight to goodbye.
I'd only ever let you go with light—
and weary—not this way, and not at night.

How could I sleep? This wasn't our routine—
if five nights-into-overnights can mean
there's ever any reason to expect
the habits of the bedroom to reflect
some finer knowing. Now our hours at brunch
seemed nothing more than alcoholic lunch,
mild warmth against a cold and empty day,
and not a way to ease ourselves away.
I knew which pillow you preferred to use,
but I had been mistaken to confuse
convenience with familiarity.

And so this morning's dawning clarity:
as daylight spreads across this cooling bed—
there is no more mistaking—I misread
your sweet, sly smile. I should have understood
goodbye-for-now had always been for good.
And so, good morning—and goodbye to this:
one lost hair on a pillow you won't miss.

Solstice I: Summer

Summer is a setup.
Maybe you never knew—
for you, it's the body
always and whoever
you touch mistaking that
touch for touching—only
a minor agony
among many.

That's why
when you are here, I play
the man who doesn't know
the other men—and you,
you don't remember them
at all.

But I wonder
what color the towel is
that he puts under you,
and whether you know how
it feels to be underneath
his sheets or what he's hung
on the wall by his bed,
and whether you've ever
claimed a side to sleep on,
or done some secret thing
you'll never do with me.

Today—the longest day—
seems too short for secrets.
You don't have to tell me
why your lips are too chapped
for summer. While we're naked,
our tattoos hide under
our skins, and our urges
can only conjure us
as we already are,
sharing nothing either
one of us wished we had.

Summer's such a setup.
It never follows through.
As the days get shorter,
I imagine winter.
And what's a scarf to you?

Solstice II: Winter

You were leaving winter
at my door—in a coat
meant for other weather—
looking for a bathing
suit, the expensive one
somebody else bought you.

Should I have pretended
to look harder for it
as if I didn't know
it was beside the bed?
Kissing my upper lip
meant less than "thank you." Your
breath still smelled like questions
we've never learned to ask,
and your mouth was swollen
with someone else's name.

Those questions are the work
of more than one season—
see me again in spring
or fall. Waiting must be
so easy when you don't
ever know you're waiting.

Morning (After) Commute

As we walk out, we could be any two
unknown, untired men.
The shirt you borrowed, just like you,
I may not see again.

We showered, and we shared some tea
before we caught the train.
But as our hands touch on the pole
between us, we abstain

from speaking, and I do not try
to interrupt your gaze
until we have to say goodbye
and start our separate days.

Such mornings tend to leave one blue
and grimy with regret.
But sharing a commute is new,
eight hours since we first met.

I'll try, then, in a day or two—
if I should feel the same—
this number that I have for you,
now that I have your name.

In the Apartment, After You've Gone

The clocks have started keeping lazy time.
The dust is slow to settle—and the air
is thick with smells I'd never known were there
when you were here. But now you're not. And I'm

left counting every leaky-faucet drop—
when I can't sleep—I press my favorite shirts
of yours, with starch, and pose them, hollow flirts
across the backs of chairs, as if a crop

of half-formed, ghostly hints of you might keep.
But each one wilts into a silent heap,
as heavy wishes will incline to fail.
Now dust will settle, and the faucet drip,
and I will stack and sort through all your mail
until you've come home from your business trip.

Second Night

I put the tea on earlier tonight.
Last night I learned you like it only hot
and bitter black. Your steeping told me that.

I scraped away the bedroom window's frost
to let the airplanes' landing lights derive
new shapes from us in shadows through the night.

I put my cigarettes away, to keep
a fresher mouth to make your mobile mouth
more likely to stay longer—and it has.

But when I called attention to the light
from airplanes landing close enough to see
us—so you said—you dried and dressed—and left—

I see it was my fault. I left the tea
for later, and you didn't know I knew
you well enough to know the dark you need.

Summer City Morning, After a Sudden Storm

The clouds that linger low arrest
our vision temporarily
as, clustered under awnings, we,
in accidental fellowship,
escape the cloudburst, sacrifice
the shelter of our streetwise solitude—

beyond our makeshift quarantine
the saturated stoops are brown
as old tobacco swells in mounds;
thin greens emerge through cracked concrete,
emboldened in the heavy air;
and bloated handbills break and bleed,
their colors streaking through the softened street—

until the clearing of the clouds
reveals a harsher light, restores
the narrow, fixed and furtive gaze
of busy city walks, as we
step out and just as swiftly dissipate.

4 a.m.

And again tonight—
this is becoming the hour
of knowing—we're two
strangers in a bed alone
together at four a.m.

There Have Been No Accidents/Injuries at This Worksite in [79] Days

What needs to shatter
when crumbling will do
a much finer job—
no pieces to glue
together, just dust,
more permanent—true?

Brief (Enough) Encounter

We collided—reading while walking, kept our
fingers keeping places inside our books and,
wishing past coincidence, scanned each other's
titles and thought not.

The Wedding Reception Ends

Tonight, he's married well—before these witnesses—
and to a future free of fear. I must be here

to recognize his happiness, the ruddy shine,
the blush that others might attribute to the wine.

His favorite song is playing as they stand; they part
to thank us separately, before they take their leave.

But when he reaches me, he's sacrificed his ease
to all those other hands. His grip is warm but weak

and brief. His wide, immobile smile displays the teeth
he's bleached, to clear the darkest stains. And then they meet

again, as if to dance. But the band stops—instead
our aphrodisiac applause sends them to bed.

He's gone. The band resumes—half sorry and half sweet—
and urges us away, toward milder happiness.

It's possible he'll pause, unwrapping gifts, to mark
the moment their first day of married time exceeds

the hours that he and I have ever known alone.
(How many of those hours could cancel all of theirs?)

My gift is not to answer—from the registry
those linen sheets will be more welcome in their home

than my first thought, a fine familiar Hermès tie—
the one I'm wearing now, the one he left behind

the latest of our nights, across my unmade bed,
unpressed, unworried, and undone, as we were then.

Aftermath

Ideal Weight

On viewing Felix Gonzalez-Torres's Untitled
(Portrait of Ross in LA), *1991. (Ideal Weight 175 lbs.)*

Remembrance is no solitary art.
So this is Ross, this multicolored mound
of candies in a heap against the wall,
to serve the curious, who cross the room
where, swindled by the promise of a sweet
distraction, as they kneel to choose a piece
then rise to peel the cellophane away,
they mimic the devotion of a prayer,
dismantling his body absently.

Whoever reads the card can understand
the sad and strange communion they have had.
But from all hands, the empty wrappers fall,
and sounds of crinkling plastic overwhelm
impatient crunches and astonished gasps,
like beetles clearing flesh from silent bone.

It's what you'd hope the one you love would do
when you have no more spirit left to stand—
collect you in the corner of a room,
to brace the fading traces of your form—
prolong, somehow—unable to forestall
the brief, indifferent sweetness of release.

Instead

There is no need to note
the pointlessness of things,
the grave utilities
of chemicals—the blood—
of all those things to come—
the wracking, wretched things—
the burning and the bile—

no—someone else will know
them all eventually
and better than you know—

no—testify instead
not of the life to come
but of bacon, the taste
of fried chicken. Speak of
chocolate—of all such things
so much farther away—
if you cannot
           say nothing.

Virginia Woolf's Pockets, Full of Stones

It was just
a simple step from the garden
like any other, the shadow,
that inarticulate spectre
whose presence you confirmed again
in the bathroom mirror, abandoned
with the falling bombs, the thunder.
As on other days, there were no
morning mortar-pestle grindings
with your coffee; yet a steady
shower of stones (count the soft thuds,
the comforting clack as they land)
was filling your pockets, and you,
you concluded, life is like this.

After

Who is getting out of bed
upstairs, when you're gone——can they
know what the morning offers
before sunlight, the body
heavy enough to drown you
under your breath?
      Where they are,
someone is always cooking,
and the curtains never close,
and dogs race across the floor
to love you, and nothing worse
ever surprises anew
with the sunrise, and the cool
air is all they need to sleep.

The Dying

And then what can you do but look
at what you were going to see
anyway—all that's no longer
there, beneath the skin or behind
the eyes? So tell another joke
to the stomach that's emptying
again, now, of almost nothing.

There is—in this wasting—muscle
enough for this—this turning out
of the pockets at the threshold.
There's nothing left for you to do
but move no muscle of your own
because all you have to bear is witness.

Pallbearers for Our Favorite Drunk

His names for us grew darker with the hour
as he released the evil of the day
until no words remained to curse us with.
We tolerated him; he bought the rounds
that fortified us as we helped him home,
sharing his weight between us, as he dragged
his heels and shuffled blind. We'd pour him through
his door, assuming somehow he'd be fine.

So when he called us to him in the end,
we came from little more than courtesy
and only stayed when there was no one else
to watch him tremble, starved—still liquid-fed,
but now a gentler diet, through the tubes
that bruised the withered arms, the heavy hands
he lifted as we tried to leave, his throat
so dry not even curses could escape.

We should have been a strange choice for this chore,
bearing his weight upon us once again—
so unprepared to offer any words,
we, who possess no knowledge of the man
beyond the steady habits of his taste
and his convenient generosity,
can only stand half-sentenced at his side,
heave him down, heaven-ward, heavier dead.

Private Room

This room's been a broken promise
we never could have kept, so long
as you were determined to live.
When you decided not to speak
anymore or eat any more
than a spoonful of whatever,
at least you had a private room
and your own bird feeders outside
that window. We promised you birds
would come and it would be the same
because they let us bring your chair.

The Death Bush

And then it was autumn
in your living room—late
autumn. Someone had brought
a bush, because flowers
had begun to gag you
just as much as food did.

Soon all the leaves turned brown
and fell, no matter what
we tried. So you started
calling it "The Death Bush"
and wouldn't let me sweep
them because why pretend
that death was anything
but an unwelcome mess.

From His Deathbed

It's over—weary with the weight
of all imaginary sins—
the leaning, closing crowd has wrapped
in turn with burning hands around—
my own—final constellation—
dark stars against the warm, awaiting light.

To Be of Use to the Dead

Finish their food.
Drink her cheap vodka.
Flush even his best pills.
Chew only his brand of gum.

> Remember the body for later.
> Pick up the check.

Buy the gifts they would have given you.
Make unexpected gifts of their things.
Wear one of his awful ties.
Tailor her coat to your size.

> Be merciful to memory.
> Untie a knot.

Cast disapproving looks on their behalf.
Take her long way home.
Quote him accurately.
Guess their passwords.

> Love someone else.
> Resume the discussion.

Pray only to their best photographs.
Invent a ritual.
Reveal a flattering secret.
Never conjure them for nothing.

                                        Abolish the inventory.
                              Astonish a chapel with laughter.

Believe in outraged ghosts.

                                        Be kind to animals—
                              because you never know.

Five Approximations of Grief

a cold bath
only your own
body warms

the certainty
that water wears
through stone

oil slowly
staining
a tablecloth

summer's strange
sun shining
anyway

a solid house
of empty rooms

At the Quaker Meeting House

The minor saints of my experience,
to whom I prayed for petty things, were there
in Notre-Dame, and I was overcome
by censered necks that lifted up their heads
just like medieval urbanites (whose dust
compacted underneath our touring feet)
did, knowing God's greatness in that He shrank
Himself to meet them, yet in shrinking great.
The stone walls held the residue of prayers—
their cold can register the smallest flames—
whose molecules He leaves in rigid place
as if to keep eternity on hold.

But in the Quaker meetinghouse, the smell
of wood, the slow decay of leaves tracked in
is sweeter, for the absence of the sweet.
Wood dulls and rots, requires constant care.
Another person's face is everywhere
and dust is all between you but the breath,
until some bidden words rise up, and fall.
Each word resounds as loudly, coming close
as it would in an echo from a stone.

When prayer passes through such simple rooms
how can I now in any house I know
avoid the expectation of a God
in gold, who weathers without weathering,
in soft wood, or the mercy of His stone?

Someone Keeps Inviting Death to These Parties

Oh, Death, since we were introduced,
we've run into each other everywhere.
I've tried to welcome you—but when I do
you act like you don't know me. Death, I'm through
with courtesy. I know your party tricks,
the way you simper and seduce—I see
how wantonly you wind around the room.
Our hostess may not know you yet—but know
I'm counting all the knives before you go,
you party-crashing, brazen early guest,
whose place some fool will always rush to set.

The Barn

Even the strong
body becomes
a rotting barn,
doors blown open
and windows rinsed
in dust. Inside
the mice outrun
the snakes sometimes,
sometimes their luck.
What you still have
of the sweet hay
of the pasture
is all this straw
that keeps you warm
waiting to burn.

Notes

The Deer Hunter. Dir. Michael Cimino. Dist. Universal
Studios Home Entertainment. 2012. Film.1978.

"Near First Avenue, After the Hurricane" evolved from a
prompt in a master class with Fanny Howe in which we
were asked to respond to a passage from the Bible, chosen
by each poet at random, in my case this passage from
Revelation 18:22.

"Ideal Weight" is a phrase drawn from the exhibition card
for Felix Gonzalez-Torres's installation piece "Untitled
(Portrait of Ross in LA)," 1991, now part of the collection
at the Art Institute of Chicago.

About the Author

Thomas March is a poet, teacher, and critic based in New York City. His poetry has appeared in *Bellevue Literary Review*, *The Good Men Project*, *Pleiades*, and *Public Pool*, among others. His reviews and essays have appeared in *The Believer*, *The Huffington Post*, and *New Letters*. Appearing regularly in *Lambda Literary Review*, his poetry column, "Appreciations," offers appreciative close readings of excellent poems from recent collections by LGBTQ poets. A Pushcart Prize nominee and past recipient of the Norma Millay Ellis Fellowship in Poetry from the Millay Colony for the Arts, he has also received an Artist/Writer grant from the Vermont Studio Center. In recent years, he has written and performed monologues at a number of venues in New York City, including Ars Nova, Joe's Pub, The Peoples Improv Theater, and Sid Gold's Request Room. *Aftermath* is his first collection of poems. Twitter: @realthomasmarch, Web: www.thomasmarch.org

About the Art

The cover image is a detail from a painting by Michael Eirhart, commissioned by the author's grandmother to memorialize a barn on the farm where she spent a crucial part of her childhood. Reprinted courtesy of Betty Marcy and the Estate of Donald J. Marcy.

About The Word Works

The Word Works, a nonprofit literary organization, publishes contemporary poetry and presents public programs. Other imprints include the Washington Prize, International Editions, and the Tenth Gate Prize. A reading period is also held in May.

Monthly, The Word Works offers free literary programs in the Chevy Chase, MD, Café Muse series, and each summer, it holds free poetry programs in Washington, D.C.'s Rock Creek Park. Annually in June, two high school students debut in the Joaquin Miller Poetry Series as winners of the Jacklyn Potter Young Poets Competition. Since 1974, Word Works programs have included: "In the Shadow of the Capitol," a symposium and archival project on the African American intellectual community in segregated Washington, D.C.; the Gunston Arts Center Poetry Series; the Poet Editor panel discussions at The Writer's Center; and Master Class workshops.

As a 501(c)3 organization, The Word Works has received awards from the National Endowment for the Arts, the National Endowment for the Humanities, the D.C. Commission on the Arts & Humanities, the Witter Bynner Foundation, Poets & Writers, The Writer's Center, Bell Atlantic, the David G. Taft Foundation, and others, including many generous private patrons.

The Word Works has established an archive of artistic and administrative materials in the Washington Writing Archive housed in the George Washington University Gelman Library. It is a member of the Council of Literary Magazines and Presses and its books are distributed by Small Press Distribution.

wordworksbooks.org

The Hilary Tham Capital Collection

Nathalie Anderson, *Stain*
Mel Belin, *Flesh That Was Chrysalis*
Carrie Bennett, *The Land Is a Painted Thing*
Doris Brody, *Judging the Distance*
Sarah Browning, *Whiskey in the Garden of Eden*
Grace Cavalieri, *Pinecrest Rest Haven*
Cheryl Clarke, *By My Precise Haircut*
Christopher Conlon, *Gilbert and Garbo in Love*
           & *Mary Falls: Requiem for Mrs. Surratt*
Donna Denizé, *Broken like Job*
W. Perry Epes, *Nothing Happened*
David Eye, *Seed*
Bernadette Geyer, *The Scabbard of Her Throat*
Barbara G. S. Hagerty, *Twinzilla*
James Hopkins, *Eight Pale Women*
Donald Illich, *Chance Bodies*
Brandon Johnson, *Love's Skin*
Thomas March, *Aftermath*
Marilyn McCabe, *Perpetual Motion*
Judith McCombs, *The Habit of Fire*
James McEwen, *Snake Country*
Miles David Moore, *The Bears of Paris* & *Rollercoaster*
Kathi Morrison-Taylor, *By the Nest*
Tera Vale Ragan, *Reading the Ground*
Michael Shaffner, *The Good Opinion of Squirrels*
Maria Terrone, *The Bodies We Were Loaned*
Hilary Tham, *Bad Names for Women* & *Counting*
Barbara Ungar, *Charlotte Brontë, You Ruined My Life*
           & *Immortal Medusa*
Jonathan Vaile, *Blue Cowboy*
Rosemary Winslow, *Green Bodies*
Michele Wolf, *Immersion*
Joe Zealberg, *Covalence*

The Washington Prize

The Tenth Gate Prize

International Editions

Other Word Works Books

Annik Adey-Babinski, *Okay Cool No Smoking Love Pony*
Karren L. Alenier, *Wandering on the Outside*
Karren L. Alenier, ed., *Whose Woods These Are*
Karren L. Alenier & Miles David Moore, eds., *Winners:*
    A Retrospective of the Washington Prize
Christopher Bursk, ed., *Cool Fire*
Willa Carroll, *Nerve Chorus*
Grace Cavalieri, *Creature Comforts*
Abby Chew, *A Bear Approaches from the Sky*
Barbara Goldberg, *Berta Broadfoot and Pepin the Short*
Akua Lezli Hope, *Them Gone*
Frannie Lindsay, *If Mercy*
Elaine Magarrell, *The Madness of Chefs*
Marilyn McCabe, *Glass Factory*
JoAnne McFarland, *Identifying the Body*
Kevin McLellan, *Ornitheology*
Leslie McGrath, *Feminists Are Passing from Our Lives*
Ann Pelletier, *Letter That Never*
Ayaz Pirani, *Happy You Are Here*
W.T. Pfefferle, *My Coolest Shirt*
Jacklyn Potter, Dwaine Rieves, Gary Stein, eds., *Cabin Fever:*
    Poets at Joaquin Miller's Cabin
Robert Sargent, *Aspects of a Southern Story*
    & *A Woman from Memphis*
Miles Waggener, *Superstition Freeway*
Fritz Ward, *Tsunami Diorama*
Amber West, *Hen & God*
Nancy White, ed., *Word for Word*

CPSIA information can be obtained
at www.ICGtesting.com
Printed in the USA
FFOW03n1943200218
45181442-45707FF